50 BURNING QUESTIONS

A SIZZLING HISTORY OF FIRE

BUS STOP

TANYA LLOYD KYI

ILLUSTRATED BY
ROSS KINNAIRD

annick press
toronto + new york + vancouver

ANNICK PRESS LTD.

Edited and copyedited by Elizabeth McLean
Proofread by Geri Rowlatt
Cover and interior design by Irvin Cheung/iCheung Design, inc.
Cover illustration by Ross Kinnaird

We acknowledge the support of the Canada Council for the Arts, the Ontario Arts Council, and the Government of Canada through the Book Publishing Industry Development Program (BPIDP) for our publishing activities.

ONTARIO ARTS COUNCIL
CONSEIL DES ARTS DE L'ONTARIO

CATALOGUING IN PUBLICATION
Kyi, Tanya Lloyd, 1973-
       50 burning questions : a sizzling history of fire / Tanya Lloyd Kyi ; art by Ross Kinnaird.

(50 questions series)
Includes bibliographical references and index.
ISBN 978-1-55451-221-8 (bound).—ISBN 978-1-55451-220-1 (pbk.)

       1. Fire—Juvenile literature.
I. Kinnaird, Ross, 1954- II. Title. III. Title: Fifty burning questions. IV. Series: 50 questions series

GN416.K94 2010   j541'.361   C2009-905786-7

Printed and bound in China

Published in the U.S.A. by	Distributed in Canada by	Distributed in the U.S.A. by
Annick Press (U.S.) Ltd.	Firefly Books Ltd.	Firefly Books (U.S.) Inc.
	66 Leek Crescent	P.O. Box 1338
	Richmond Hill, ON	Ellicott Station
	L4B 1H1	Buffalo, NY 14205

Visit our website at **www.annickpress.com**

To Matthew

Acknowledgments

The author thanks Elizabeth McLean for guiding this manuscript, and Pam Robertson for her input on earlier versions of the work.

Table of Contents

It's the latest stick, sir, on special today.

Gathering around the Fire

WHAT DO YOU PICTURE when you think of fire? A fire truck wailing down the street, a warehouse blaze on the evening news, or a water bomber sweeping over a burning forest? Usually, we see fire as a destructive force that can threaten homes or even lives.

But fire is not only something to fear. Its energy surrounds us all the time, wherever we are, giving us light, heat, and cooked food. If we stopped to think about the flames in our world—fires that have built civilizations, sparked religions, and literally changed the surface of Earth—imagine how many questions we might have.

Thousands of years ago, people believed fire was one of the basic elements of the universe, and they made up stories to explain the mysterious force. People today are still fascinated by fire, and the 50 questions here will probably spark many more of your own.

Fire!

Chapter 1

THE SPARKS OF CIVILIZATION

When humans learned to use fire, it wasn't just because they craved barbecued meat. Fire allowed people to protect themselves from wild creatures, stay warm in cold climates, and hunt entire herds of mammals. This new ability to control flame changed…everything!

Question 1
Who's for dinner?

SCIENTIST ROBERT BROOM was digging around in a South African cave in 1947 when he found an old skull. A human skull.

Broom called his archeologist friends and they flocked to the site with their tiny picks, spoons, and brushes. Soon, they whisked away the dirt and found the remains of thousands of years of—dinner. With each layer, they revealed animal bones and tools, mixed with charcoal from the camp fires of ages past. They could almost picture a tribe of ancient humans crouched around the flames, roasting an antelope leg.

Then the archeologists hit a layer that dated from more than 1.5 million years ago. These remains didn't include charcoal, because humans hadn't yet learned to use fire. The scientists noticed something else, too. Instead of animal bones chewed by humans, the cave now contained human bones gnawed by lions!

Until they controlled fire, humans were the prey.

Flash Fact
Scientists disagree about when early humans first used fire, but the evidence found so far suggests that people began to harness it between 1.4 and 1.6 million years ago.

let's get a pizza!

Question 2

Who's faster—
a Cub Scout
or a cave kid?

IMAGINE YOU'RE WATCHING a Cub Scout rub two sticks together to make a spark.

You're waiting.

Waiting.

Still waiting

It takes forever, right? Well, it might take a long time for an inexperienced Scout, but not for fire experts many thousands of years ago. They had so much practice, they could do it in minutes.

Around the world, people developed unique fire-sparking techniques. In Australia, they sawed one piece of wood back and forth across the other. In the South Pacific, they used a stick like a miniature plow, pushing it along a groove. And in Africa, people twirled a stick between their palms, resting the end on a flat piece of wood.

In a race, these folks would beat a Cub Scout every time.

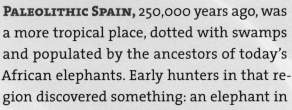

Question 3

Was roasted tortoise the first one-pot meal?

PALEOLITHIC SPAIN, 250,000 years ago, was a more tropical place, dotted with swamps and populated by the ancestors of today's African elephants. Early hunters in that region discovered something: an elephant in a swamp can't run very fast. With its legs caught in deep mud, the animal was easy to kill, and everyone could feast for a week.

So, how to get more elephants stuck in more mud?

Hunters lit long lines of fires in the brush behind elephant herds, driving them toward the swamps. Then, when the big animals were trapped and couldn't run or attack as quickly, hunters with spears and clubs surrounded them.

All around the world, other early people used fire to hunt. Some tribes on the east coast of North America set fire to the forests once each year. This drove deer and other game to the shore, where they could be killed and the meat dried for winter. Other groups smoked rabbits out of their warrens, or lit strings of prairie fires to herd buffalo toward cliffs. In Venezuela, people burned the meadow homes of tortoises. When the grass fires went out, the tortoises were dead—and perfectly cooked for dinner.

What's cooking?

gone cold

WOULD ANYONE CARE for some Marinated Spiced Carp? If this fish dish sounds delicious, you could whip some up using a recipe from China, written down more than 3,000 years ago. It's the oldest recipe ever found.

The first cooked foods were probably barbecued—roasted over open flames. But many early societies invented ovens as well. The earliest pit ovens date from well over a million years ago in Africa and 300,000 years ago in Europe. Depending on what part of the world people lived in and what rocks and tools were available, the ovens were constructed in different ways. In Hawaii, people lit bonfires in pits and heated volcanic rock. Then they buried a pig on top of the hot rocks until it was roasted. In Australia, people wrapped a kind of bread dough in large leaves and baked it over coals.

The invention of cooked food may have led to evolutionary changes. According to some scientists, teeth became smaller, because cooked food was easier to chew. People also grew taller and larger, because the food was easier to digest.

It's 3,000 years old!

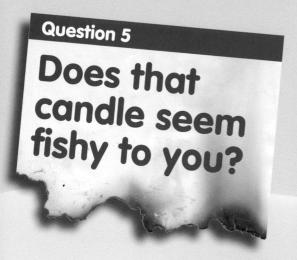

Does that candle seem fishy to you?

WHEN EARLY EUROPEANS created their first cave paintings 32,000 years ago, they worked by the light of primitive candles—hollowed stones filled with animal fat. Scientists know this because they've found those stones still inside the caves, and still blackened by smoke. Today, we can only imagine trying to paint by the light of such flickering, smoky, and stinky lanterns!

About 3000 BC, the Egyptians improved things a little by adding flammable plant stalks to the fat—the first known candlewicks. It was the Romans who are credited with creating the first "real" candles about 2,000 years ago, by dipping a wick into fat again and again. Finally, people in the Middle Ages replaced animal fat with beeswax, though only rich folks could afford these sweet-smelling versions.

Around the world, candles have been made with many things, from bayberry extract to paraffin, a wax made from petroleum. Native people along the Pacific coast of North America came up with an especially simple and ingenious light—they put a stick through the body of a fish called an oolichan, or candlefish. These fish are so oily they will actually burn like a candle.

BRIGHT BLUBBER

In Greenland and Nunavut, in northern Canada, Inuit people used soapstone lanterns with two compartments—one for seal or whale blubber, and the other for dry moss or lichen, which was used as tinder to light the lantern. These lamps were used for light and heat, and even as a cooking surface. Until the early 20th century, every Inuit mother tended a lamp, gathering enough fuel each fall to feed the flame through the long northern winter.

THREE CRAZY WAYS TO MAKE A CANDLE

1. POKE A STICK THROUGH AN OILY OOLICHAN.

Watch it!

2. LIGHT A PAT OF YAK BUTTER.

Yak Butter

Yak toast

3. BOIL A WHALE, SCOOP UP THE OIL, AND ADD A WICK.

ACTIVITY!

Lantern Light

Lanterns were a big improvement over candles. They didn't flicker as much, you could use them outside in the wind, and they were brighter. The first street lanterns were candles enclosed in glass domes, hung in London in 1417 to make the evenings safer.

Here's how to make your own tabletop lantern. You'll need to ask an adult to supervise.

You need:

- a clean tin can with the label removed
- a strip of paper long enough to wrap around the can
- duct tape or packing tape
- a pen or pencil
- a nail
- a hammer
- a tealight candle

What to do:

▶ Fill the can almost to the top with water, then freeze it. This will keep it from denting when you bang the nail through.

▶ Wrap the paper all the way around the can and tape it in place.

▶ Draw a simple picture on the paper using dots, with the dots quite close together.

▶ Carefully, use the hammer and nail to puncture the can at every dot.

▶ Remove the paper and allow the ice to thaw, or hold the can under warm water until the ice melts enough to fall out.

▶ If the ice has buckled the bottom of the can, gently hammer it flat.

▶ Light a tealight candle inside your new lantern!

How do you warm a wigwam?

No one knows exactly when people switched from gathering and nurturing coals from forest fires or lightning strikes to actually creating their own fires. But archeologists believe that once humans learned to spark flames, they soon planned cooking and heating fires for their own shelters. Some of the first people to use fire in individual homes were probably tribes in the Mediterranean. Around the world, other early homes were designed with hearths in mind. The stone homes of Crete, the sod-roofed houses in ancient Britain, and the wigwams and tepees in North America all featured central openings from which smoke could escape.

Keeping those home fires burning made chilly winter nights seem a lot warmer. Suddenly, mountain slopes and northern forests that had once been too cold for survival became new hunting grounds. By about 11,000 years ago, humans were even living in northern Siberia, within the Arctic Circle.

Party at my place!

OW!

THE FIRST FIRE

According to a native legend told along North America's Pacific coast, Gray Eagle once ruled the world. He hoarded fire, keeping it for himself and his family. But Raven saw fire hanging on the wall of Gray Eagle's lodge, and he stole it. Carrying it in his beak, he flew it down to the humans, who had been struggling in darkness. After his heroic flight, people could use fire—but Raven's wings turned black forever, singed by the flames he'd carried.

How do you squeeze fire from a stone?

FIRST, YOU NEED a type of quartz called flint, plus a rock that contains a mineral called iron pyrite. Next, you hit your flint against your rock and if you're lucky—really lucky—you get a spark. Many thousands of years ago, this discovery "sparked" some ideas. It was way faster than rubbing sticks together! Once steel took the place of rocks (between 2,000 and 4,000 years ago, depending on where you lived), sparks flew even faster. People started carrying little pieces of flint and steel when they traveled.

By the time Europeans settled into the first villages, a flint and steel rested beside every hearth. And hundreds of years later, European gentlemen still carried miniature versions in their pockets to light their pipes. Each tiny tinderbox held flint, steel, dry material called tinder to catch the spark, and a tiny wick to keep it burning.

Even today, flint-spark lighters are used by welders and chemists. If they're working under dangerous conditions, carrying one of these mechanical lighters is safer than carrying flammable butane gas.

Do not play with rocks! You will start a fire!

IT'S A MATCH!

1680 ROBERT BOYLE RUBS A SULFUR-COATED STICK IN PHOSPHOROUS.

1827 JOHN WALKER COATS WOODEN STICKS WITH CHEMICALS AND MAKES THEM BURST INTO FLAME.

1828 SAMUEL JONES MAKES SMALLER VERSIONS FOR SMOKERS.

1831 CHARLES SAURIA GETS RID OF THE STINK BY USING POISONOUS WHITE PHOSPHOROUS.

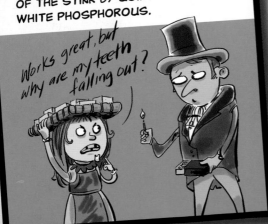

1847 JOHAN EDVARD MASS-PRODUCES THE FIRST SAFE MATCHES.

PHOSSY JAW

When 19th-century smokers bought their supplies, it was the matches—not the cigarettes—that should have carried health warnings. Early matches used a poisonous mineral called white phosphorous. People's gums swelled, their teeth fell out, then their jaws became infected and started rotting away. Talk about a horrible case of ashtray breath!

White phosphorous was also bad news for the teenage girls who sold matches on city streets. After balancing their merchandise on their heads for a year or two, these "match girls" ended up bald. Meanwhile, workers—including child laborers—breathed poisonous fumes as they made matches in their homes or in factories. By the early 1900s, public campaigns had ended the use of white phosphorous on both sides of the Atlantic.

Flash Fact
Today, people use 500 billion matches each year.

🙰 **HOT CAREER** 🙰
MOVE
BE A MATCH GIRL

Your hair might fall out
Your teeth might fall out
Your jaw might drop off

20213146

Chapter 2

BURNINGS AND BLESSINGS

yum!

As fire became central to human life, some people began to worship fire gods. These could be huge, angry deities or friendly spirits who protected home and family. Sometimes the same god exhibited both extremes, in an ancient case of mood disorder. Even today, many religions incorporate fire—through candlelight services, incense burning, or even funeral cremations.

Would you like Agni when he's angry?

HINDU PEOPLE BELIEVE that the god Purusha was killed by the other gods. As he died, Purusha fell, and his enormous body created the world. One of his eyes became the sun, his brain became the moon, his navel became the air, and his feet became Earth. As his last breaths left him, they formed two new gods: Indra, the god of storms and thunder, and Agni, the god of fire.

Agni grew large and powerful, inhabiting every corner of this new world. He became the electricity in lightning, the spark of life in every creature, and the sap that moves through plants. He hid inside wood, but people could see his sparks when they rubbed sticks together.

Agni was a protector, offering warmth and light. But he was also dangerous, occasionally destroying forests or villages. Some people imagined him like a lion who raced through the woods with his orange mane flying behind him, leaving smoke and ashes in his wake.

Fire gods around the world shared Agni's dual qualities—warmth and danger.

Don't talk to him until he's had his coffee.

Burnings and Blessings   17

WHO'S THE HOTTEST FIRE GOD?

- In Eastern Europe, Svarozhich was the warmth of summer, the god who ripened the corn. But if you spit into a fire, he'd bring you a lifetime of bad luck.
- In ancient Persia, Atar could be a fierce destroyer. Yet he accompanied the sun across the sky.
- Japan's Ho-Masubi gave people warmth and light, the power to forge metal, and the ability to cook food. If he was neglected, though, he could char an entire village with lightning speed.

How do you want your village, medium or well done?

Does anyone still worship fire gods?

THERE AREN'T MANY FIRE-WORSHIPPERS around these days. But many religions do use fire as a symbol. For some, a candle represents comfort, like the warmth of a fireplace in winter or the friendliness of a camp fire. Others feel that the pure energy of fire reflects the purity and greatness of God. Or people might light candles because they believe that as the candle burns away, the smoke carries their prayers up to heaven.

In some homes and churches, flames are lit to remind people of miracles that happened long ago. Jewish people light candles during their annual Hanukkah celebrations to remember that once, in 165 BC, there was only enough oil in the Temple of Jerusalem to keep the temple's eternal flame burning for one more day. Amazingly, the flame burned for eight whole days—the exact length of time it took for the people to prepare new oil.

Flash Fact

The miracle in the Temple of Jerusalem is celebrated in Jewish homes around the world with a special candle holder called a nine-branched menorah. One candle is lit on the first day, then an additional candle is lit each day for the eight days that the sacred flame burned.

Orthodox Christians celebrate another apparent miracle—a recurring one. Each year on the day before Easter, the archbishop in Jerusalem recites a prayer. Then he carries an unlit olive oil lamp into the tomb of Jesus, while people outside chant and pray. When he emerges from the tomb, the lamp is always burning.

BURNING FOR LOVE

One of the most extreme ties between fire and ritual lies in the Hindu practice of *sati*. This tradition involves a woman throwing herself on the funeral pyre of her husband, or sometimes being forced onto it, and burning to death. *Sati* has existed for more than 2,000 years. When the British tracked the practice in India in the early 1800s, they estimated that about 600 women were cremated alive each year.

Some say that by sacrificing herself, a *sati* widow becomes a goddess called a *satimata*. She proves her devotion, purifies herself of any wrongdoing, and guarantees a reunion with her husband in the afterlife. But many people, including Hindus, say the rite takes advantage of grief-stricken women, and even allows families to avoid having to care for a widow by forcing her to her death.

Public campaigns to ban *sati* began in the 1830s, and the practice is now extremely rare.

I've been invited to a barbecue!

What's the deal with the barbecued lambs?

DOES BURNING UP MONEY for dead ancestors or roasting food for gods seem a little strange? After all, only living people can actually spend money or eat food. But humans have given burnt offerings for thousands and thousands of years.

In China, some people believe that by burning paper and money, they can send it to the spirit world. Every year as winter approaches, the faithful burn paper clothes or money to help their dead ancestors "survive."

And all over the world, people have burned food for gods, for all sorts of reasons:

- Send the gods food, and they will grow stronger.
- Show the gods devotion, and they will send a good harvest.
- Toss a feast on the fire, and the gods will have a party and forget to bother humans.

People have tried to please gods by burning grain, lambs or calves, and even people. Between the 13th and 16th centuries, the Aztecs were famous for their mass human sacrifices. They boiled prisoners, tore out their hearts, or roasted them alive.

You might think that's horrifying. The Aztecs thought they had no choice. They believed that if they didn't sacrifice enough people, the sun would fail to rise.

THE NATIONAL BANK OF BURNED BODIES, LTD.

The sun god Huitzilopochtli lived for 52 years, then died and came back to life, over and over again. The Aztecs believed they had 52 years to accumulate sacrifices. If Huitzilopochtli didn't receive enough human blood during that time, he wouldn't have the strength to rise from the dead. The world would stay dark forever. Those Aztecs took their job seriously. Anthropologists believe they killed at least 20,000 victims each year.

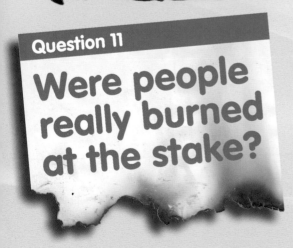

Question 11

Were people really burned at the stake?

IN THE 15TH CENTURY, Spain was a cosmopolitan place peopled by Muslims, Jews, and Christians. But a rise in anti-Judaism and a quest for land and power prompted the Catholic queen, Isabella, and her husband, King Ferdinand, to decide to "purify" their country. They wanted to rid the land of Jews, Muslims, and even non-Catholic Christians and Catholics whose families had converted from Judaism. Few were safe.

The royal couple created a court called the Inquisition, and it was a truly nasty piece of work. The guy in charge was named Thomas de Torquemada. He believed there were only two ways to deal with non-Catholics: torture them until they gave up their beliefs or burn them alive. He killed about 9,000 people, tying them to poles called stakes and setting them on fire in public squares. According to the Inquisitors, burning their victims was done partly to "cleanse" them and partly to warn others. As a bonus, the king and queen got to keep their victims' land and cash.

Torquemada wasn't the first person to burn people at the stake, and he wasn't the last. From the 1400s to the 1700s in Europe, witch burnings were common. Often, "witches" were healers or herbalists or midwives. If someone they treated died, or if the crops in their village failed, these people became convenient scapegoats. In the 300 years that witchcraft trials were common, at least 40,000 people were killed.

Flash Fact

Witch-hunts still occur today in some parts of the world. And in a few rural regions of India and Africa, witches can still be burned at the stake.

GIRL POWER, MEDIEVAL STYLE

In the 15th century, France was a mess. King Charles VI was insane, and England had invaded. Then the daughter of a French farmer began to receive what she said were visions from God, instructing her to drive the foreign army out of France. Dressing in boys' clothes so she could travel more safely, Joan of Arc managed to meet and impress Charles VII, an heir to the French throne.

Joan donned armor and led the French army in several victorious battles. But when she was captured, her family couldn't pay the ransom demanded. Then the English charged Joan with heresy, or acting against the beliefs of the church, because church authorities did not believe that an ordinary peasant could communicate directly with God. Meanwhile, Charles VII ignored her plight, not wanting to be caught in the scandal.

Joan was found guilty, tied to a stake in a public square, and burned alive. She was 19 years old.

Why don't firewalkers get toasted toes?

VILLAGERS DIG a long, deep pit in the ground. After lining it with round river stones and building a huge bonfire on top, they wait. When the fire has burned down to coals, the rocks are red-hot. A small piece of cloth tossed into the pit will burst into flames.

The firewalkers emerge from a nearby hut. They trot single file to the pit and walk briskly across the coals. When they finish with no blisters, no burns, no marks of any kind, they know they have earned the grace of the gods.

There are firewalkers around the world, almost always men, in places as far apart as Greece, Fiji, and Sri Lanka. They've drawn the attention of scientists, who have created two possible explanations for the amazing phenomenon. The first theory is that even though the coals are tremendously hot, a thin layer of moisture on the soles of the feet protects the firewalkers. The second is that the burning coals are very small, and small surfaces don't give off large amounts of heat.

But people who have witnessed fire-walking doubt both explanations. Occasionally, firewalkers who lose their concentration are burned. Why would this happen if their feet were protected by water or if the coals weren't producing high levels of heat?

Those who believe in the spiritual side of fire-walking say that firewalkers have risen above the power of flame. Their faith in their abilities or in the protection of the gods is so strong that it allows them to achieve an altered state—a state stronger than the hottest fire.

Don't try it in flip flops!

FIJIAN FIRE MASTERS

On Beqa Island in Fiji, people believe that hundreds of years ago, a strong young man discovered a tiny humanlike creature trapped in a hole in the river. The man quickly rescued him. In gratitude, the creature taught him to be more powerful than fire. For as long as the sun rose and set, the creature promised, the man and his male descendants would be able to walk on coals.

Perform Your Own Magic

Show your friends your magical powers by sending your breath right through a glass jar. You'll need a real flame for this experiment, so ask an adult to supervise.

You need:
- a candle
- a container such as a glass jar, taller than the candle

What to do:
▶ Light the candle.
▶ Place the candle behind the glass jar.

▶ Sit in front of the jar, so the jar is between you and the candle. Blow against the container.

Did the flame go out? Did your breath magically pass through the container?

Well, not really. Air (or wind) tends to follow curves, so your breath goes around the container to put out the flame.

Do other fire-related marvels have scientific explanations, or are they truly miraculous? Scientists and historians can't agree, so you'll have to decide for yourself.

Chapter 3
WHEN FIRE GOES TO WORK

BUS STOP

Potters, blacksmiths, miners, chefs, taxi drivers, pilots, astronauts, firefighters, and stockbrokers. What do these people have in common? Their jobs all involve fire, from the raging heat of the forge to the tiny spark that powers a cell phone.

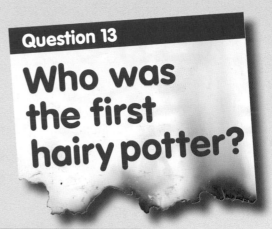

Who was the first hairy potter?

THE FIRST PERSON to make pottery may have lined a fire pit with clay, then discovered that the clay was hard and waterproof the next day. Or someone might have lined a basket with clay, set the basket down near a fire, and returned to find a new waterproof container.

However they discovered it, people in eastern Europe started making ceramic pieces more than 27,000 years ago. In China, pottery was in use at least 18,000 years ago. All around the world, from Japan to Egypt, the Middle East, and the island of Crete, people made different styles of dishes, urns, and goblets. Carrying water and cooking food became easier than ever before.

Is there any pottery in your kitchen cupboards? It was likely made in the same way that ancient artisans would have made it—by molding clay, then baking it in a very hot oven, called a kiln.

Who were the first blacksmiths?

Six thousand years ago, metalworkers in Sinai, Egypt, built waist-deep, stone-lined pits. Two holes in the stone walls allowed air to be blown in through pipes to feed a blazing fire. In this simple furnace, artisans placed a small amount of copper ore and charcoal over searing hot embers and managed to achieve temperatures of more than 1000°C (1830°F). This process, called smelting, created a stronger metal.

In other parts of Africa, people smelted ore by mixing it with charcoal in a long, low pit. They enlisted the help of insects, by filling an old, hardened termite nest with fire, then pulling it over the pit until the ore below melted and bonded. By studying ancient tools, archeologists can tell that some tribes were smelting metal at least 8,000 years ago.

CAUTION: VULCAN AT WORK

In ancient Greece, people believed the steam escaping from the tops of volcanoes was the smoke from the god Vulcan's forge. Vulcan was in charge of crafting weapons for Ares, the god of war, and thunderbolts for Zeus, the king of the gods.

I wish they would hurry up and invent glass!

How do you make a rock transparent?

THE MESOPOTAMIANS WHO LIVED in what is now the Middle East were the first to discover this trick, about 4,500 years ago. They melted a mineral called silica, found in rocks, and created a clear, syrupy liquid. Then they mixed the molten silica with a mineral made from ashes, called potash. They heated the concoction in a kiln. When the stuff cooled, it was hard and transparent—in other words, glass.

By 1500 BC, people all around the Mediterranean were making glass in long strands and then wrapping the strands into bottles or rounding them into beads. Glassmakers also used molds to make containers.

Two thousand years ago in Syria, craftspeople learned to attach a blob of glass to a long metal pipe. By blowing into the other end of the pipe, they could inflate the glass, creating something that looked like a soap bubble. Through practice and experimentation, they learned to manipulate the shapes of these "bubbles," and were soon making elaborate cups and vases, in the same way artists make them today.

This will get the kids clean.

OTHER HOT DISCOVERIES:

- oven-baked bread
- salt crystals from boiled seawater
- soap, made from ashes and animal fat

How can fire and steam move a locomotive?

IN THE LATE 1600s, scientists began experimenting with steam. If they boiled water, then kept the steam under pressure, they found they could use the pressurized steam to move things. Things like gears. Here's how they moved things "full steam ahead":

1. Boiled water creates steam.
2. The high-pressure steam flows into a metal cylinder.
3. The steam moves a metal hammer, or piston.
4. The piston rod attaches to metal rods outside.
5. The metal rods turn a gear.

Power! As soon as the energy of steam became the energy of motion, inventors used it to drive weaving looms, water pumps, and eventually even ships and trains.

When Fire Goes to Work   **33**

When is an engine fire a good thing?

IN AN INTERNAL COMBUSTION ENGINE, a mixture of air and gas takes the place of steam. Released in tiny portions, then lit by sparks, the mixture explodes into the cylinder, moving a piston hundreds of times per minute.

These new, more powerful engines ran the first experimental automobiles as early as the 1860s. They were also used by all sorts of industries. Miners pumped water from mine shafts, smelting companies switched from coal or wood fires to gas furnaces, and railways sent locomotives across entire continents.

All these things are still fueled by internal combustion engines today. Fire is hidden deep inside the machines, providing the power.

Flash Fact

Want to move at jet speed? A jet engine is a type of internal combustion engine that sucks in air and compresses it. When gas and a spark are added… boom! Because the explosion is forced backward, the jet is propelled forward—fast.

Does NASA really "fire" rockets?

IMAGINE ENOUGH LIQUID OXYGEN to fill 11 tanker trucks. At the Kennedy Space Center in Florida, that's how much is stored at one end of the rocket launch area. At the other end, there's the same amount of hydrogen. When a space shuttle is ready to launch, the two gases flow into a divided tank below the rocket. At the last moment, workers remove the divider and a spark of electricity ignites the gas.

Boom! The explosion is big enough to blast the rocket through Earth's atmosphere.

As flames shoot into the sky, the extra heat, smoke, and fire are directed down into an enormous brick and concrete trench, where they can't harm the launch machinery. Meanwhile, masses of water are pumped onto the launch pad to contain the flames, prevent sparks, and muffle the overwhelming noise of the explosion.

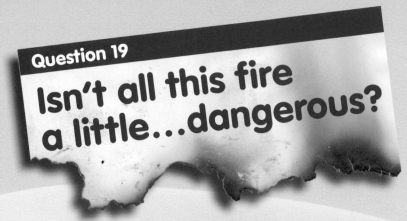

Isn't all this fire a little...dangerous?

ENGINES WERE SPARKING industrial changes long before they were thrusting rockets into space. In the late 1800s and early 1900s, the amazing power of these new machines resulted in something called the Industrial Revolution. People left their farms and small, cottage-based businesses and poured into the cities to find better-paying work. In cities throughout Europe and North America, workers crowded shoulder to shoulder at factory tables. Outside on the streets, the roofs of houses leaned toward one another, almost touching. These quickly growing cities were breeding grounds for a new kind of danger—industrial fire.

On a Sunday night in 1666, flames from a London bakery fire tore through ramshackle row houses, spreading from neighborhood to neighborhood. There was pandemonium in the streets. Drumbeats

and ringing church bells warned citizens. Families scurried back and forth, trying to move their belongings through dark, smoke-filled alleyways. There was no fire insurance in 1666, so anything lost would be gone forever. The mayor led the first fire-fighting efforts, without success. The king's brother took over, commandeered soldiers and sailors, and battled for three days until the city's entire water system ran dry. Finally, five days after the fire began, the winds dropped and workers managed to contain the flames. King Charles II ordered all new buildings to be made of stone and brick, so fire could never threaten the city again.

Our 21st-century streets may be better protected and our firefighters more practiced, but industrial fires remain viciously dangerous. Before 2000, the sleepy city of Enschede in the Netherlands was home to a fireworks warehouse that had existed for 30 years without attracting attention—the mayor didn't even know that fireworks were stored in his city. Then, a small fire inside the warehouse spread outside, setting trucks and storage containers ablaze and causing a series of explosions that flattened the factory and the neighborhood. Twenty-two people were killed, including four of the firefighters who had responded to the blaze.

FAMOUS FIRE DISASTERS

- **1871.** Chicago's entire business district was destroyed after a fire tore through crowded slums and industrial land, then blazed toward the city's landmarks. About 17,500 buildings burned, and almost a third of Chicago's residents were left homeless.

- **1881.** Two thousand opera fans were gathered at Vienna's Ring Theatre when flames enveloped the building. Almost 800 people died, unable to escape. The government of Austria closed every theater in the country while it reviewed fire regulations. Many theaters in the rest of Europe did the same.

- **1911.** In New York City's Triangle Shirtwaist Factory, hundreds of young women sewed side by side. When fire broke out, there was no escape—the bosses had locked the doors to make sure the women didn't leave work early. After 145 people died, labor groups demanded better working conditions and better fire regulations across the United States.

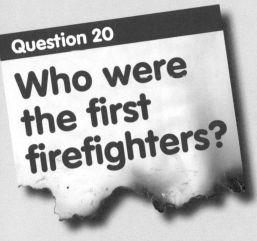

Who were the first firefighters?

MORE THAN 2,000 years ago, Roman Emperor Augustus created a crew to walk the city streets and watch for signs of fire. If they spotted flames, citizens would quickly help fill and carry buckets of water to douse the blaze, knowing their own homes and businesses were at risk.

Methods didn't change much until the Great Fire of London in 1666. After that, private insurance companies took charge of training crews and arranging for hand pumps to throw more water at sudden blazes.

In 1824, the first modern fire department was founded in Edinburgh, Scotland. When a ringing church bell or a yelling messenger boy signaled a fire, crews would rush to the scene. The men pumped water by hand from the city pipes, working in teams and switching every few minutes so that fresh muscles could keep the water flowing. Other workers hoisted ladders to reach burning rooftops, while still others cleared debris from the area.

only over your mouth!

Flash Fact
Early firefighters were sometimes called smoke-eaters. They wore long beards so when they were working in thick smoke, they could pull the hair over their mouths and filter the air.

When Fire Goes to Work   39

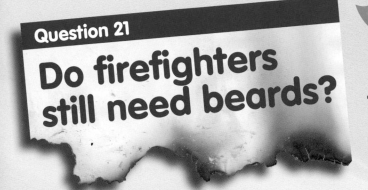

Question 21

Do firefighters still need beards?

THE FIRST HORSE-DRAWN water pumps were used in the mid-1800s. The world's first "modern" fire engine started dousing blazes in 1907, using a single motor to run both the vehicle and the water pump. Soon, vehicles were carrying water tanks and hoses, extendable ladders, and hammers to break down doors.

Today's firefighters wear hoods, gloves, and boots made of fire- and heat-resistant materials. In place of the "smoke-eater's" beard, each worker is equipped with a self-contained breathing apparatus— a tank of air worn on the back, attached to a face mask. Still, even with all this advanced equipment, fire-fighting is one of the most difficult and dangerous jobs in the world. Researchers have found that firefighters' hearts beat at maximum speed in the heat of a blaze. It's not surprising! Wouldn't your heart race?

All Fizzed Out

Firefighters know that there are three elements to a fire: fuel, heat, and oxygen. In other words, if you take away the wood, the spark, or the air, there's no fire. You'll be using real flame in this activity, so ask an adult to help.

You need:

- 2 handfuls of baking soda
- a shallow bowl
- a small candle, such as a tealight
- a small glass of vinegar

What to do:

▶ Spread the baking soda evenly over the bottom of the bowl.

▶ Place the candle in the center of the bowl, and light it.

▶ Slowly, pour the vinegar into the baking soda, making sure you don't splash the candle.

Did your flame go out? Can you figure out why?

The vinegar and baking soda fizzed together to create a gas called carbon dioxide. This new gas took up all the space at the bottom of the bowl, leaving no room for oxygen. And without oxygen, the flame couldn't burn.

Chapter 4

FIRE TALK

Have you ever seen a camp fire flickering in the distance? Or watched an emergency flare blaze on the side of a highway? On a dark night, flames can be spotted across a valley or over the open ocean. That's why, thousands of years ago, they served as communication devices. In fact, camp fires were the first text-messaging systems. All around the world, long before cell phones or e-mail, armies and hunting parties relied on fire to help exchange information. One puff of smoke = be right back = brb!

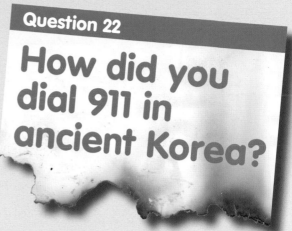

How did you dial 911 in ancient Korea?

IMAGINE YOU'RE KING TAEJO, ruler of Korea in the 1300s. Your palace is in the capital city, far away from the coast. But Japanese raiders keep attacking from the shores of the Yellow Sea, 400 kilometers (250 miles) to the west. How do you protect your people?

1. Pray hard.
2. Send messengers who run really fast.
3. Make gargantuan smoke signals.

King Taejo went for option number three. Hundreds of years before the first telephone lines, he found a way to quickly send signals back and forth across his country. Soon, 673 fire beacons stood on hilltops, ready to send simple codes. During the day, guards watched for columns of smoke. At night, they could see the light from the flaming pyres. When raiders were spotted, King Taejo would know how many, and from what direction.

Why hasn't anyone called?

Flash Fact
Some of King Taejo's fire beacons still survive. In Seoul, the capital city of Korea, five of them perch on the hillside like enormous beehives.

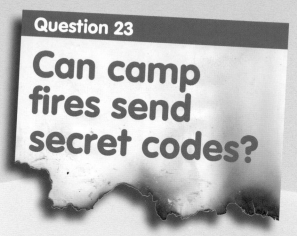

Question 23

Can camp fires send secret codes?

THE ANCIENT KOREANS weren't the only ones heating things up. In the 1500s, European visitors saw the Yaghan people at the tip of South America use smoke signals. They wanted to gather a large group by the shore, where a beached whale provided enough food for many families.

Far to the north, on the Great Plains of North America, native groups knew that a puff of smoke could be seen for great distances. Using a blanket to alternately fan and smother a fire, people made sequences of smoke puffs.

These smoke signals often weren't used with formal codes, because codes could be cracked or interpreted by enemy groups. Instead, families and friends would agree on signals.

Some tribes, such as the Apaches, used more complicated forms of code. In a row of fires, the number of smoke columns and the size of each column might mean different things. At night, the Apaches even used flaming arrows shot into the air to send messages. Signals could be sent according to the number of arrows, the distance between them, and the patterns they formed as they flew.

SMOKE SNAFU

More than 2,000 years ago, a Greek historian named Polybius wrote about fire signals and codes, and about how useful they were during wars. But Polybius also described their weakness—only very simple messages could be sent.

What if a sender wanted to say something complicated, maybe that he'd discovered a spy? So Polybius invented a new system using 10 torches. Creating various patterns, a sender could use a sort of torchlight alphabet. History doesn't tell us if Polybius's system was ever actually used, though.

BY LAND OR BY SEA

Paul Revere waited in the dark, across the river from Boston. It was 1775 and he belonged to a group of Americans planning a rebellion. The British weren't too happy about that idea, and intended to capture the leaders in a surprise attack. But Paul Revere knew their secret. The only thing he didn't know is whether the British would come over land or from ships. And so he stood, watching for a friend to send him a signal.

There—a flash in the night sky. Another! His friend had climbed a clock tower and shone a lantern flame two times. That meant the British would cross the river to attack.

Paul leaped on his horse and galloped through the countryside, stopping at farms and villages along the way to shout a warning.

He arrived in the city of Lexington in time to warn the rebel leaders. Thanks to the prearranged fire signal, people were armed and ready when the British soldiers arrived. And so the first battle of the American Revolution began.

Are fire signals used today?

A SIZZLE OF MAGNESIUM and a brilliant burst of light. Emergency flares help soldiers, lost hikers, and rescue workers. In our age of satellites and wireless Internet, it's a little surprising to discover we still use fire signals. But on a dark night, they're sometimes the best way to attract attention.

A soldier in the desert can set off a flare to show a plane where to drop supplies. A search plane in the Arctic might drop one to blaze over the ice, looking for stranded sailors. A submarine can launch a special underwater flare to illuminate the surrounding ocean. Sometimes, a burst of flame can do what a GPS (Global Positioning System) can't.

FLASH!

SOS

What if you were lost in the woods? You could try lighting a fire and fanning a blanket over it to create three puffs of smoke—that's the code used by Canadian and American scouting organizations to signal danger. You could build three fires side by side. Or send a smoky SOS—three short smoke puffs, three long, three short. To a passing plane, those messages would spell "Trouble down here—send help!"

Spy Games

Can you use a flashlight to send your own secret messages? This activity works best in a dark room. Try it in the evening, or in your basement with the blinds closed.

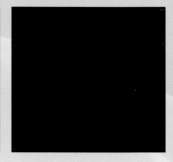

You need:

- 2 flashlights
- 2 pieces of cardboard or black construction paper
- a friend

What to do:

▶ Send your friend to the other side of the room and turn out the lights.

▶ Hold your cardboard over your flashlight beam to block the light. Then slide it up and down to make your beam of light flash.

▶ Try sending an SOS message in Morse code— three short flashes, three long flashes, then three short again. Can your friend understand it?

▶ Now let your partner try.

▶ Can you and your friend create a code of your own? What might two long flashes and three short ones mean? What about five short flashes? See if you can communicate in the dark using only your flashlights.

Where was the first lighthouse?

FIRE CAN BE USED to communicate with those at sea as well as with those on land. The first lighthouses were tall stone towers with stone or metal baskets on top to hold fires. They guided sailors in the Mediterranean Sea more than 2,500 years ago. One marked the strait between the Black Sea and the Mediterranean. Others guided ships into Athens' harbor, and more marked the shores of Italy, Spain, and France.

The most famous lighthouse in the ancient world was built by Ptolemy I, pharaoh of Egypt. Every day, ships carried spices, cloth, and wine into Alexandria, and left with cargo holds full of papyrus, medicine, jewelry, and perfumes. But it could be hard to see the port entrance at night, let alone navigate around the nearby bluffs and sandbars. When the lighthouse—the Pharos of Alexandria—was finished after 20 years, it rose nearly to the height of a 40-story building. Only the Egyptian pyramids were taller. It boasted three stone tiers, with the top tier holding a blazing fire. Slaves lugged load after load of wood up spiraling stairs to keep the beacon burning.

It's light work.

Flash Fact
The Pharos of Alexandria was one of the seven wonders of the ancient world. It was destroyed by earthquakes in the 1400s, but divers found remains of the famous structure in 1994.

OVERBOARD IN LAKE ERIE

Lighthouse keepers had to be hardy, independent sorts. Many lived alone for most of the year on isolated points and islands. Some even acted as single-person rescue crews, as in the famous case of Frederick Hatch, a lighthouse keeper on Lake Erie.

In 1890, a storm bashed a barge against a port breakwater in Cleveland, Ohio. After tugboats failed to pull the barge into the harbor, Frederick set out on foot along the top of the breakwater. He threw ropes to several sailors and pulled them onto the breakwater, but one last sailor and the captain's wife were still clinging to the mast of the barge.

Frederick launched a lifeboat and managed to reach the stranded pair. Then, just when they had all climbed onto the tiny craft, a huge wave swept them overboard. With the sailor and the woman clinging to him, Frederick grabbed a rope and pulled them all hand-over-hand to safety.

How do lighthouses work today?

IN THE 1700s, lighthouses were lit with whale oil lanterns. Kerosene gas was used in the late 1800s. Today, it's electricity. The lantern inside a modern lighthouse is an intense electric light, focused by rotating lenses. Many of these lights flash in particular orders, so sailors can determine their ship's location by watching for the pattern.

Lighthouses are often equipped with radar transponders that send out electromagnetic waves. Nearby ships will receive beeping dots on their radar screens to indicate the presence of danger.

There aren't as many lighthouses as there used to be. Keeping those big lamps burning is expensive, and most modern ships have such good navigation equipment that lighthouses aren't as necessary. Around the world, more and more lighthouses have become automated beacons, without the lighthouse keepers who once worked so hard to keep the shorelines safe.

What's a lightship?

Wanted:
One sailing crew willing to live on the deck of a small ship anchored off the English coast, near London. When storms arise, crew members will rope themselves to the deck, brave the lashing winds and mighty waves, and keep two oil lanterns lit to warn other ships of the surrounding sandbars. Anchor chain may occasionally break, sending ship into the swells of the open ocean. Wages available upon survival.

PEOPLE ACTUALLY DID THIS JOB in the 1700s! The first lightship was anchored near the estuary of the Thames River in England, and ship-wrecks decreased dramatically. The United States followed England's example, and in the early 1800s, 56 lightships were on duty off the Atlantic coast.

By the middle of that century, new floating marker buoys and beacons meant the lightships were no longer needed, and adrenaline-seeking sailors had to search for new adventure.

Chapter 5
ALL FIRED UP

Why do people talk about being hot and bothered, getting fired up, or feeling smoldering passion? Why do we put candles on the dinner table to signal romance, or set flags on fire in protest? Obviously, flames can be more than a tool for everyday needs such as warmth and cooking. They can serve as a means of expression, too. All over the world, people use fire as a way to show the "heat" of their emotions.

How do you "spark" a romance?

Darling, my heart's on fire.

IT'S A SCIENTIFIC FACT. When people feel physical attraction to each other, they breathe faster. Their heart rate increases. Blood flows more quickly through their body. Humans feel "hot and bothered" because they actually *are* hot.

LANTERN LOVE

As the first full moon of the Chinese New Year rises in the night sky, people in China and Korea celebrate the Lantern Festival. They take to the streets with elaborate paper lanterns. This is a time for joy and playfulness, and also for matchmaking. In the past, upper-class girls who spent most of their lives indoors would emerge onto the streets, hoping to attract a suitable husband. Professional matchmakers hurried through towns comparing horoscopes and destinies, to determine the best matches. Even today, many parents in the two countries give their children more freedom during the evening festivities, hoping they might find love.

When is fire most frightening?

In the 1920s, the Ku Klux Klan, or KKK, had more than 100,000 official members across the United States. They believed that white Protestant Christians were naturally superior, and that the problems of the world were caused by "outsiders" and minorities. They targeted black people, Jewish people, new immigrants, and Catholics.

KKK members terrorized and sometimes murdered their targets, and one of their most frightening symbols was a burning cross, supposedly a reminder of the intensity of the KKK's religious faith. Dressed entirely in white, with hoods over their heads to appear more terrifying—and to hide their identities—men would gather outside a victim's house, erect a giant cross, and light it on fire in the middle of the night, often chanting racial slurs, vandalizing property, and threatening the people inside.

Membership in the KKK dwindled by the 1930s, yet Klan organizations still exist, particularly in the American South.

THROW ANOTHER BOOK ON THAT BLAZE

In another part of the world, a different extremist group also turned to fire. They were called the Nazi Party, and Adolph Hitler was their leader. In 1933, inspired by a hate-filled speech at a Nazi Party rally, young Germans in 34 cities tore books by Jewish and "un-German" authors off library shelves and used them to build enormous bonfires in the streets. In their minds, they were using fire to "purify" German literature.

Mein Kampf

Flash Fact

After a massive 1937 art show designed to mock paintings they found offensive, Hitler's deputies burned up to 1,000 works by expressionist and other modern artists.

I've had bad reviews before, but this is ridiculous!

TALK ABOUT A GUY who couldn't share! In the second century BC, Emperor Shi Tuang Ti united ancient China. He changed the system of government, announced new laws and punishments, and created his own school of philosophy called legalism. He was so confident in this new system that he outlawed all other competing philosophies, especially the ideas of a philosopher named Confuclus.

Burn the books or bury the writers?

When 460 scholars disagreed with him and were found to own banned books, Shi Tuang Ti had them buried alive. He then burned every "old-style" book in his kingdom, keeping only one copy of each for his personal library. Oh...and he ordered his personal library burned when he died.

While Shi Tuang Ti's efforts to unite the country were successful, trying to wipe out Confucianism was a big fat failure. People all over Asia still follow the tenets of that philosophy.

Why burn bras and draft cards?

BURNING AN EVERYDAY OBJECT can sometimes transform it into a symbol of protest. During the Vietnam War in the 1960s, when thousands of American men were drafted into the army whether they wanted to fight or not, burning a draft card became a way to speak out against both the war and the government.

In 1968, around the same time that men were burning draft cards, a group protesting the Miss America beauty pageant in the United States wanted to show the world what they thought about society's expectations of women. They threw hairspray bottles, high-heeled shoes, makeup, and bras into a garbage can. What happened next is a bit of a mystery. Newspaper reports said that the women lit the garbage can on fire. But some of the protesters said they were going to set it on fire until the police stopped them.

Either way, the protesters made an impact that day. Decades later, women's rights activists are still occasionally labeled as "bra-burning feminists."

FLAG-RANT MISUSE OF FIRE?

In 1984, a young American activist named Gregory Lee Johnson marched through the streets of Dallas, Texas, as part of a political protest, and set a United States flag on fire. The state court found him guilty of vandalism, fined him $2,000, and sent him to prison for a year. Johnson appealed the decision all the way to the Supreme Court. There, the judges ruled that his act of flag burning was a part of having free speech, a right of every American, and overturned his sentence.

Still, many Americans consider flag burning a betrayal of one's own country. And in places such as Denmark and Finland, the courts agree. In those nations, it's illegal to burn flags, and protesters must find other ways to express their views.

Flash Fact

In 1906, a South African law required Indian and Chinese residents to register with the government. Mahatma Gandhi encouraged people to burn their registration cards, one of the first protests in the life of the famous nonviolent activist.

Why do arsonists set fires?

ARSONISTS ARE PEOPLE who set fires on purpose. These fire setters are usually male, and researchers suggest that up to half of them are angry and looking for revenge. Their girlfriends have broken up with them, their bosses have fired them, or their parents have punished them.

Perhaps more frightening are the arsonists who are *not* motivated by revenge. A small number of fire setters—about 1 in 10—love the thrill and the power they feel by starting a fire and watching it grow. These people don't need anger or thoughts of revenge to spur their actions. They just need opportunity.

Flash Fact

The opposite of an arsonist is someone with pyrophobia. People with this irrational fear are terrified of flames and feel as though they're in constant danger of being burned.

How do you catch an arsonist red-handed?

YOU DON'T. WELL, NOT OFTEN. It's difficult to even confirm arson as the cause of a blaze. Did someone accidentally drop the lit cigarette that sparked the pile of garbage by the wall and started the house fire? Or did someone intentionally hold a lit cigarette to a piece of paper in the pile of garbage until the pile was ablaze?

Arsonists do get caught sometimes, though. In California in the 1980s, investigators began to think one man was responsible for a series of fires. The device used to spark the blazes was always a simple arrangement of matches and a fuse, difficult to trace. But the fires seemed to be set whenever a conference on arson was held in the area. At last, after a single fingerprint was found at one of the crime scenes, police began tracking a suspect. John Leonard Orr worked as a fire investigator with the Glendale Fire Department—a fire detective turned arsonist! The police arrested him in 1991 and he was sentenced to life in prison.

BLACK SATURDAY

Flames turned Australia's southeastern forests to ashes in 2009, killing more than 170 people and countless animals. There were so many fires raging on February 7 that year—about 400 individual blazes—that Australians named the day Black Saturday.

Extremely dry weather contributed to the fires, but investigators believed that some were deliberately lit, an act the Australian prime minister called "mass murder."

Flash Fact

Fire investigators watch for clues. If a fire started in more than one place at the same time, or if the ashes contain a gasoline or chemical residue—those are signs that a blaze might have been deliberately set.

Detective Duty

A fire has destroyed Lightning City Music Club. You're the fire investigator called to the case. Can you discover the cause of the blaze?

You need:

• a blank piece of paper

What to do:

▶ Cover the clues on the following page with your blank paper.

▶ Slide the paper down to reveal one clue at a time.

▶ Continue until you guess the cause of the fire. Then check the bottom of the page to see if you're right!

The Clues:

Witnesses tell you that people started running from the music club as the fire alarm sounded. At the same time, flames began shooting from the roof.

The ceiling of the club was coated in soundproofing insulation. It's now black and crispy.

Heavy curtains once hung behind the stage. Now they're in tatters.

The stage itself is totally destroyed. The band—Lightning Heavy Metal Makers—escaped, but their instruments are melted and twisted.

The remains of two lightning-making machines lie charred at the back of the stage.

The Answer:

Have you guessed? The lightning machines lit the stage curtains on fire. The flames raced up the curtains to the ceiling, then reached the roof in minutes.

A fire like this one destroyed a nightclub in Rhode Island in 2003. Fire investigators built a complete replica of the club to learn how the fire spread so quickly.

Chapter 6

READY, AIM, FIRE!

People have been fighting with fire for almost as long as they've been playing with it. Fighters have burned enemy storehouses so winter food would run short. They've sent flaming arrows onto thatched roofs, setting villages alight. They've burned the forests around their own towns, so their enemies couldn't hide in the underbrush.

In modern times, our strategies for fighting with fire have grown more and more…inflammatory. Now we use bombs instead of flaming arrows and burn entire jungles instead of single storehouses. Increasingly, people are beginning to wonder if fighting fire with fire is such a good idea.

Who threw it first?

ABOUT 2,900 YEARS AGO, soldiers in the Middle East filled clay pots with coals and hurled them at enemy soldiers. It worked so well, armies across the region searched for ways to throw bigger flames farther. By 360 BC, the Greeks were using catapults. Now soldiers could hurl pots of burning pitch from Mediterranean harbors to land on the decks of enemy ships. Because ships of the time were built entirely of wood, fire was the most dangerous weapon.

THE ARCS OF ARCHIMEDES

Archimedes was a mathematical genius, fascinated by numbers and shapes. When the Roman army invaded his home city of Syracuse, Sicily, in 212 BC, he invented machines to stop them. They included towering cranes to drop rocks on enemy soldiers, huge claws to lift ships out of the water, and cannon-like machines to hurl rocks through the air. But perhaps his most innovative machine was a massive parabolic reflector to focus the sun and set ships on fire.

No one knows anymore if Archimedes' reflector worked, but some scientists think it's possible. This type of curved and mirrored surface collects and concentrates the sun's rays into a dangerous, laser-like weapon. A modern version in France is used to melt iron and produce steel.

Could workers in the third century BC have created a reflector precise enough to turn the energy of the sun into a powerful weapon? We might know for sure if Archimedes had lived to record the whole story. Unfortunately, he was captured by Roman soldiers, and when he told them not to touch his papers, he was killed.

Just Row!

Ow! This flame throwing is a terrible idea!

What is Greek fire?

PSSST...DID YOU HEAR? *Those guys in Constantinople are into some bad stuff, man. They're using flamethrowers. Seriously.*

That was the rumor over a thousand years ago, when the Greek army unleashed a new weapon, said to be the invention of an architect named Kallinikos. Using pumps and long metal tubes, soldiers shot a kind of flame that seemed supernatural—it couldn't be extinguished with water. Armies across the Middle East quivered in fear of this new "Greek fire."

The actual formula for Greek fire has been lost to history, but today's scientists believe it was a mixture of pine resin, sulfur, and petroleum. The concoction would have been thin enough to pump through a tube, yet thick enough to keep burning as it flew through the air. Like a grease fire on a modern stove, the pitch would have been water resistant. Splashing it would have only splattered the mixture and spread the flames.

FONDUE, CONSTANTINOPLE STYLE

In 674, Arab troops surrounded Constantinople and held the people captive. Then, a mysterious figure named Kallinikos sneaked into the city with a secret formula. Soon, Greek fire was raining down upon the Arab forces, and Constantinople was free.

Greek fire rescued Constantinople again in 941, when Igor the Russian attacked the harbor with thousands of ships. Fifteen fire ships came to the city's defense, shooting flames from cannons. The Russian ships blazed. The sailors and soldiers leapt into the sea, where their heavy armor pulled them into the depths.

Cannonball!

Question 36

Would you like some gunpowder in your stew?

CHINESE WOMEN WERE THE FIRST to use saltpeter, a white chemical that sometimes appears on the surface of the earth. Two thousand years ago, they used it as a spice, throwing a little into the pot when they were short of salt.

Maybe it was the wife of an alchemist who spilled a bit of saltpeter on the cooking fire itself. Pop! Pop! Pop! The bursts of noise and light were harmless, but intriguing...

In the ninth century, alchemists searching for a formula to turn ordinary metals into gold or silver, and for an elixir to guarantee eternal life, began experimenting with the substance. They never found the secret of creating gold or cheating death—but they invented something that still delights people today. By scraping charred wood into a fine dust, then adding saltpeter and sulfur, they could create small explosions. They called their creation "fire chemical" or "fire drug" and used the earsplitting bangs and showers of light to entertain nobles and emperors.

Hit the Deck!

Gunpowder explodes because of a chemical reaction—something that happens when one substance is mixed with another, and the result is an entirely new substance...or three. Can you make your own "explosive" chemical reaction?

Because this experiment makes a mess, it's best done outside.

You need:

- safety goggles
- film canister, or other small plastic container with a tight-fitting lid
- 20 mL (1½ tbsp.) vinegar
- a piece of tissue
- 5 mL (1 tsp.) baking soda

What to do:

▶ Put on your safety glasses. (Vinegar in the eyes stings.)
▶ Pour the vinegar into the bottom of the film canister.
▶ Spread the tissue over the top of the canister, make a small well with your finger, and place the baking soda in the center. Don't let the tissue touch the vinegar below.
▶ Snap on the lid, and flip the canister upside down on the ground.
▶ Stand back!

Did your film canister explode? Vinegar is an acid, and baking soda is the opposite of an acid—something called a base. When this acid and base mix, they cause a chemical reaction that creates water, sodium acetate, and carbon dioxide. The bubbling carbon dioxide blows the canister off its lid.

Who invented guns?

CHINESE EMPEROR Jen Tsung began using gunpowder in weapons in 1044. His small "grenades" and gunpowder-wrapped arrows caused more light and sound than actual damage, but they were perfect for scaring the pants off his enemies.

In 1233, gunpowder grew more dangerous. Chinese soldiers began carrying long, paper tubes filled with fuel and gunpowder. When they lit these fire lances, flames would shoot forward more than a body length. A generation later, bamboo tubes replaced the paper ones. And soldiers learned to fill the tubes with pellets, peppering their enemies with the world's first bullets.

WARNING: PRODUCT MAY EXPLODE

The Mongols conquered China in 1274. They seized control of the gunpowder factory, fired the old scientists, and sent in their own men to figure out the new invention. Unfortunately, the new researchers hadn't attended any firearms training courses. In 1280, some finely ground sulfur caught fire. The workers thought it was amusing, and only halfheartedly tried to put out the flames as they spread toward a store of fire lances. Soon, the blaze was out of control. It reached an arsenal of bombs and the entire workshop exploded, killing 100 workers and 200 families who lived nearby. The blast was so loud, people thought an enemy army was invading.

Flash Fact

Although there were a few explosions along the way, the Mongols quickly became gunpowder experts. They made the first cannons and the first metal guns in the early 1300s.

That worked!

Didn't his mother tell him not to play with fire?

SWEDISH CHEMIST ALFRED NOBEL was trying to perfect an explosive made from an oily chemical called nitroglycerin. If handled carefully and lit in exactly the right way, nitroglycerin could be 10 times stronger than gunpowder. It could blast train tunnels out of solid stone, or blow enemy soldiers to bits.

Then in 1864, while Alfred was at a meeting to gather new research money, his younger brother Emil blew up the laboratory. In an explosion that shook nearby buildings, shattered windows, and obliterated the research lab, Emil and four other researchers died instantly.

Stockholm's city leaders said, "No more nitroglycerin!"

But Alfred was obsessed, and entrepreneurs wanted this superchemical. He set up a new lab on a barge just outside the city limits. Orders poured in from railroad builders in North America, miners in Australia, and weapons factories in Europe.

Unfortunately, Alfred had missed one important fact. His invention became less stable the longer it aged and it could explode spontaneously.

Only one year after his barge business opened, tragedies occurred around the world. Ships sank and warehouses blew up. In San Francisco, a leaking crate of nitroglycerin detonated on the docks, killing 10 people and turning an entire city block to rubble. Alfred's own factory on the barge, plus a second one, exploded.

But Alfred still wouldn't quit.

After several years, he learned how to mix nitroglycerin with clay to create dynamite, five times stronger than gunpowder, safe to store, and easy to use in tunnels and tight spaces. By 1874, his factories were producing shiploads each year, and Alfred was rich.

FROM BAD TO GOOD

As Alfred grew old, he thought more about all the deaths his inventions had caused. Determined to leave something good for the world, he created a fund that would reward achievement in the fields of physics, chemistry, medicine, literature, and peace. We now know these annual awards as the Nobel Prizes.

Is it raining fire?

FIRST HUMANS LEARNED to hurl fire, then shoot it from tubes...and it wasn't long before they were dropping it from the sky. By the early 20th century, scientists had created the bomb. Filled with explosives and fuel, these fiery containers could burn up forests, mountainsides, or entire neighborhoods.

In World War II, both German and Allied forces used fire bombs. In London, so many bombs fell for so many days between 1940 and 1941 that the time became known as the Blitz, a name taken from the German word *blitzkrieg*, meaning lightning war. On one day alone, bombs sparked 2,000 fires that destroyed 5,000 homes.

Flash Fact
A bomb causes a huge rolling wave. Some experiments have shown this wave to be twice as hot as molten rock.

What's napalm?

DOES THIS SOUND LIKE mad scientists at work? Researchers mixed a chemical called naphthalene with another chemical called palmitate, and added it to gasoline to make a gooey gel. A gel that caught fire really, really easily. In fact, it was designed to coat and burn everything it touched.

They called their fire gel "napalm," and napalm bombs were first used by American pilots in France at the end of World War II. But the United States made napalm infamous when it developed a longer-burning version called napalm B and dropped tons of it during the Vietnam War in the 1960s and early 1970s. So many people were hurt or killed that, in 1980, the United Nations passed an agreement to ban the use of napalm on civilian targets. In other words, no more throwing fire gel at innocent people.

The United States did not sign the UN agreement, but claimed in 1991 to have destroyed all its napalm stocks. Then, in 2003, the U.S. Army admitted to using a napalm-like substance in Iraq. Their continued use of this sort of chemical weapon has brought criticism from around the world.

FLEEING THE FLAMES

In 1972, a young girl named Phan Thi Kim Phúc fled her village in South Vietnam, the skin seared from her back by a napalm attack. Her escape was captured in an image by photographer Nick Ut. Ut's photo was published in newspapers around the world and he eventually received a Pulitzer Prize for it. Phan Thi Kim Phúc survived the attack on her village but endured years of surgeries and burn therapy. She moved to Canada in 1992, where she has spent much of her adult life working to help children harmed by war.

Question 41

How do you put out an oil well fire?

In 1991, the United States went to war to protect Kuwait, one of its major oil-trading partners in the Middle East. When Iraqi forces had invaded the tiny country, they'd met little resistance. But when they faced 400,000 U.S. soldiers and 200,000 from other United Nations countries, the Iraqis soon retreated.

The Iraqi army exacted a devastating revenge as they left. They set more than 700 oil wells on fire.

An oil well fire can't be put out with a simple spurt of water—even if water were easily available in the middle of the Kuwait desert. For months, the oil wells burned. The entire country was covered in black clouds of smoke, and the pillars of flame could be seen from space.

Eventually, workers dug huge lagoons to supply seawater. Then expert firefighters used explosives, chemicals, or liquid nitrogen to suck up the available oxygen, dousing the flames for long enough that water could cool the equipment. With the help of crews from the United States, Canada, China, France, and Hungary, all the wells were capped after nine long and dangerous months.

Flash Fact
The smoke from Kuwait's oil well fires was detected in the snow of the Himalayan mountains and in the air above Hawaii, on the far side of the world.

Chapter 7
A FIERY PLANET

To the ancient people of the Hawaiian Islands, volcanoes were mystical forces with awesome powers. When lava flowed from mountaintops, people thought that the goddess Pele was angry. In ancient China, people believed that the world was perfectly peaceful until the fire god and the water god fought, creating the first volcanoes. And in Greece, lightning bolts were seen as the weapons of Zeus, ruler of all the gods.

Today, we know that volcanoes and other fiery forces of nature have scientific, not mythical, explanations. But that doesn't make them any less exciting or more predictable. Despite our most advanced research, we still can't control a volcanic eruption, a lightning strike, or even a wildfire.

Why do I feel like I'm floating?

WE'RE ALL FLOATING! Earth's crust—the solid ground we walk on—is resting on a layer of hot, melted rock called magma.

In a way, the ground is like the hard chocolate coating on a dipped ice cream cone. Imagine that you've bitten into the cone, just once, and the chocolate has cracked into large chunks. Those chunks are like the "plates" of solid ground that cover Earth. Their edges never seem to quite meet properly. And where they bump together, a little bit of ice cream—or, in Earth's case, a bit of magma—seeps through.

Along the borders of the continental plates, where they jostle against one another, the pressure of the magma beneath sometimes builds until the fiery liquid rock is forced upward, creating a volcano.

Do not eat the planet!

HOT AS MOUNT ST. HELENS

When Washington State's Mount St. Helens blew its top in 1980, the cloud of gas over the new crater was hot enough to broil meat or melt tin. Lava poured down the mountainside, destroying forests, bridges, railroad tracks, and long swaths of highway. The amount of energy released by the mountain equaled 27,000 atomic bombs.

Is that a great ball of fire in the sky?

OUR BUBBLING SUN IS SO BIG that a million Earths would fit inside it. It's so intense that it releases more energy in a second than all the humans on our planet have used in 100,000 years. Now that's hot!

If the sun were a normal fire, like a camp fire, it would have used up all its fuel millions of years ago. Yet scientists estimate that it's been steadily burning for 4.6 billion years. The secret lies in the incredible pressure at the center of the sun. The pressure makes tiny particles called atoms constantly collide and break, releasing energy. In the center, temperatures reach 2.2 million°C (4 million°F). Searing hot gases rise toward the sun's surface, where they cool slightly, then circle back down, like heat waves in a giant oven.

Does our sun have acne?

WHEN ITALIAN SCIENTIST Galileo peered through his telescope, he discovered dark patches on the surface of the sun in 1610. When other scientists began observing these "sunspots," they found that Earth became colder as the number of sunspots temporarily dwindled. Researchers now believe that decreases in the sun's activity could have caused past ice ages.

The largest sunspots are bigger than Earth itself. As the number of spots increases, so do solar flares. These massive explosions are caused by unstable magnetism on the sun's surface. With the power of a billion megatons of dynamite, they send burning gas shooting into space. The effects of this sort of discharge reach Earth in minutes, as the radiation hits our atmosphere in a phenomenon known as a geomagnetic storm. Radio waves are skewed and satellites slow down.

Researchers are still studying our sun, and they're beginning to believe that spots and flares affect more than we know. Dolphins and whales, for example, may not be able to navigate as well during disruptions of the atmosphere. And so many homing pigeon races have gone awry during geomagnetic storms that organizers now check for solar flare activity before beginning their events.

Don't try this at home!

it's the latest model.

Are lightning bolts the weapons of Zeus?

LIGHTNING STRIKES EARTH about 100 times each second. If we could capture the energy in just one of these jolts, we could keep a light bulb burning for three whole months.

This type of electricity is all about static. Storm clouds build up a big negative electrical charge—one that's different from Earth's positive electrical charge. In a lightning storm, the clouds send down charged "feelers" toward the ground. When they get close enough... zap! The different charges meet, creating a channel of electrical fire between cloud and ground. Around the bolt, the air grows five times hotter than the surface of the sun. And the air vibrations caused by all that heat roll out as thunder.

Lightning can take different forms. The most common is an electric flash inside a cloud or between two clouds. The type most people have seen is fork lightning—the spectacular bolts that appear to sear down from the sky. A third kind is called ball lightning, and it's one that scientists still don't understand. These globes of fire appear most often during thunderstorms, and sweep over the ground, hover in the air, or even roll around inside buildings. They're so rare that they're extremely difficult to study.

Opposites Attract

This experiment creates static electricity, the same force that attracts negatively charged lightning to the positively charged ground.

You need:

- a balloon
- a wool sweater
- running water
- a string
- a piece of O-shaped cereal

What to do:

▸ Standing next to a wall, rub your balloon quickly back and forth against the wool sweater. Slowly, hold your balloon against the wall. Does it stick?

▸ Stand near a running faucet. Rub your balloon quickly against the wool, then hold it near the running water. What happens?

▸ Tie one end of your string to the O-shaped cereal, and suspend the other end from a doorknob. Make sure the cereal doesn't touch the door.

▸ Rub your balloon quickly against the wool, then hold it near the cereal. What does the cereal do?

Everything around us is made of microscopic particles called atoms. Each atom has a nucleus surrounded by electrons, like a sun surrounded by planets. When you rub wool against a balloon, the balloon picks up extra electrons, giving it a negative charge, like lightning. Now it will attract things with neutral or positive charges—things like the wall, a stream of water, or a piece of suspended cereal.

YES! PEOPLE WHO have been struck once are more likely to be struck again—if they survive the first time. About 20 percent of lightning victims die. The other 80 percent suffer symptoms that range from serious burns and difficulty breathing to numbness, weakness, and memory loss.

No one knows why people struck once are at greater risk. *The Guinness Book of World Records* calls an American park ranger named Roy Sullivan the "human lightning rod" after he survived a record number of strikes. He was hit seven times between 1942 and 1977, suffering injuries such as burns and the loss of his eyebrows.

Another interesting news flash: four times as many men as women are struck by lightning each year. That *could* mean that electricity likes men best. Probably, it means men are more likely to be outside during thunderstorms, either working, fishing, or swinging metal golf clubs.

Flash Fact

The Empire State Building in New York City is struck by lightning about 100 times a year. Fortunately, it's protected by metal rods that channel the electricity safely to the ground.

Nice game of golf, dear?

DANGEROUS LIGHTNING EXPERIMENT, 1752 VERSION

BENJAMIN FRANKLIN RUNS OUTSIDE IN A LIGHTNING STORM.

HE UNFURLS HIS KITE. LIGHTNING STRIKES THE KITE, BENJAMIN FRANKLIN TOUCHES A METAL KEY AND GETS A JOLT.

EUREKA! LIGHTNING IS MADE OF ELECTRICITY.

DANGEROUS LIGHTNING EXPERIMENT, 1753 VERSION

RUSSIAN PROFESSOR GEORG RICHMANN READS BENJAMIN FRANKLIN'S BOOK.

HE RUNS OUTSIDE IN A LIGHTNING STORM. HE UNFURLS HIS KITE.

HE'S STRUCK BY A SPINNING GLOBE OF BALL LIGHTNING, AND FRIES.

Are those giant matchsticks?

IN CITIES, WHERE fire departments stand ready, storms don't usually cause too much damage. But in the wilderness, lightning can be devastating. It often strikes far from trails and roads, making it difficult for firefighters to reach the flames. Each year, lightning is responsible for an average of more than 12,000 wildfires in the United States and over 3,600 are reported in Canada.

There's another major cause of forest fires—people. Carelessness causes thousands of wildfires each year. People leave their camp fires unattended or only partly extinguished, or throw lit cigarettes into the brush, burning up great patches of woodland.

In May 1987, a worker cutting brush in China's Great Black Dragon Forest spilled a little gasoline on the forest floor. Then, when he pulled the starter cord on his machine, a spark ignited the gas. Within moments, the dry forest floor was alight. Working frantically with shirts and blankets, his crew tried to smother the flames. But it was no use—the fire seemed to roar away from them in every direction.

Although more crews raced to save the woodland, dry conditions and high winds fed the flames. Desperately, firefighters fought to clear an area of brush around an ammunitions cache used by the Chinese military. They succeeded, but lost the battle to save the nearby city of Xilinji. Smoke choked the streets as residents fled. One group of firefighters, working to evacuate 200 residents, were so blinded by smoke that men had to walk in front of the fire trucks, guiding them down the roads. Miraculously, they only lost one truck. The firefighters and the 200 citizens survived.

The Great Black Dragon Fire burned for more than a month. When cooler weather finally arrived, the flames had scorched an area larger than Scotland.

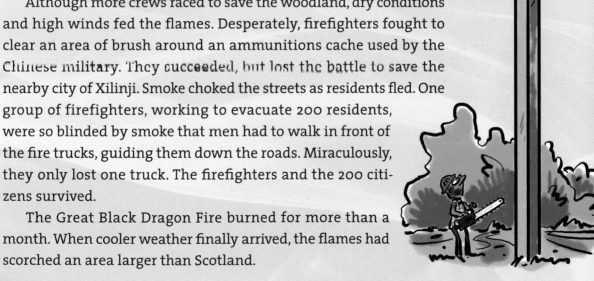

Where's the fire?

Do racoons carry fire extinguishers?

FOREST FIRES SEND ANIMALS fleeing and firefighters scrambling. In Canada, government agencies spend up to $500 million a year on fire control. They train work crews, load helicopters and jets with water and fire retardant, and even drop firefighters by parachute into hard-to-reach areas. And in the United States, fire suppression costs billions.

But while firefighters make great efforts to protect valuable land and keep fire away from towns and cities, scientists have learned that sometimes nature can extinguish a forest fire better than people can. In 1998 in Yellowstone National Park, lightning storms created a string of uncontrolled blazes. About 25,000 firefighters and 4,000 soldiers arrived from across the continent to help battle the flames. But no matter how hard they worked, the fires kept burning.

They blazed for more than three months. And when they were finally put out, it wasn't the work of firefighters. The park's first snow arrived on September 11 to snuff out the fires.

Flash Fact
In June 1940, lightning started 1,488 fires in Montana in only 10 days. That's one hot world record.

TOUGH TENTS

When fighting forest fires, workers carry heat-resistant tents in their packs. These tents are made of aluminum and fiberglass and look like space-age foil caterpillars. Because they can reflect 95 percent of a fire's heat, they can be used as emergency shelters if workers get trapped by flames.

This sort of shelter is a last resort, and can't always withstand the force of a blaze. But the shelters have saved at least 300 people in the United States since firefighters began carrying them in the 1970s.

Question 49

Is a forest fire ever a good thing?

ALTHOUGH FOREST FIRES are incredibly destructive, they leave behind open space, fertilized soil, and fresh young growth to feed wild animals.

In western North America, lodgepole pines drop cones year after year, but many of the cones remain dormant. They just sit on the forest floor, their seeds locked in tiny chambers sealed by hardened pitch, called resin. Until...fire! In the heat of a forest fire, the resin melts, releasing the pine tree seeds onto the forest floor. Fertilized by the ashes, baby pine trees are soon springing up all over.

Other trees and creatures benefit from fires as well. Aspen, ponderosa pines, and Australian grasstrees are all designed to weather a wildfire or two, and even thrive afterward. After the 1998 fires in Yellowstone National Park, researchers discovered that elk, snowshoe hare, lynx, and predatory bird populations eventually benefited from the blazes, thanks to new, open meadows and better hunting grounds.

How about a fire-charred log as a cozy crib? That's how some bugs think. Fire beetles can sense heat across entire valleys. When they detect a wildfire, they head toward the charred areas to mate and lay their eggs. There, among the still-smoldering coals of burned logs, the larvae can hatch without competition from other bugs.

Fire beetles aren't the only creatures that love a good blaze. By counting songbirds, researchers have discovered that there are actually more birds in recently burned forests than in untouched woodland. Why? It's a simple food-chain effect. Fires mean dead wood. Dead wood means wood-eating bugs. And more bugs mean more bug-eating birds.

oh darling, it's perfect!

Burn! Baby, Burn!

ONE SHRUB'S QUEST FOR PERSONAL SPACE

The greasewood bush loves open spaces. To get enough room to "branch out," this North American plant has developed techniques to actually hasten forest fires. As it matures, it drops small, dry sticks—like kindling—around its base. Meanwhile, its leaves produce more and more flammable oil. When lightning strikes, the bush is ready to help spread the flames! After a fire has passed, the plant's deep roots send up new seedlings, specially adapted to grow quickly from the ashes. They even sprouted after nuclear bombs were tested in a Nevada greasewood habitat called Yucca Flat in 1962.

In the Embers

SINCE ITS EARLIEST USE, fire has drawn people together on cold nights. In New Zealand, the Maori once gathered around the flames to hear the cycle of stories that explained their world. The Iroquois people of eastern North America held their highest councils around blazing bonfires, praying and dancing around the fire as agreements were reached or wars were declared. For the Inuit of arctic regions, a central fire in each tent or igloo made it possible to exist through cold, sunless winters, to work and to sew, and to gather together for stories or dances.

Even today, campers gather around fires to eat or share tales. Fireworks festivals each summer bring neighbors out of their individual homes to celebrate together. The warmth and light of fire naturally brings people closer.

Can we live without fire?

WHEN WE HEAR THE RUMBLE of the furnace starting in the morning, turn on the burner of the gas stove, or light the candles on the dinner table, we're using fire in the same ways early humans did hundreds of thousands of years ago—for heat, cooking, and light. When we eat off ceramic dinner plates, walk across a concrete floor, or gaze through a glass window, we're using materials formed by flame.

Fire affects how we eat, how we dress, how we see, and how we travel. Without it, we would have no light bulbs, no cars, and no computers. Our furnaces would be silent and cold. Millions of years after humans learned to control flame, it's present in every moment of our lives.

Could we live without it? Well, humans lived without it about 1.5 million years ago. But back then, they were eaten by lions for lunch.

A Fiery Planet   **93**

Further Reading

Goodman, Edward C. *Fire!* New York: Black Dog & Leventhal
  Publishers, 2001.

Gorrell, Gena K. *Catching Fire.* Toronto: Tundra Books, 1999.

Kenney, Charles. *Rescue Men.* New York: PublicAffairs, 2007.

Masoff, Joy. *Fire!* New York: Scholastic, 1998.

Newton, David E. *Encyclopedia of Fire.* Westport, CT: Oryx Press,
  2002.

Thompson, Lisa. *Battling Blazes.* Minneapolis: Compass Point Books,
  2008.

Wagner, Rob Leicester. *Fire Engines.* New York: Metro Books, 1996.

Bibliography

Appenzeller, Tim. "The Coal Paradox." *National Geographic*. March 2006: 98.

Beddoes, J., and M. J. Bibby. *Principles of Metal Manufacturing Processes*. London: Arnold, 1999.

Brown, Stephen R. *A Most Damnable Invention*. Toronto: Viking Canada, 2005.

Callick, Rowan, and Pia Akerman. "Police track arsonists responsible for Victoria bushfires." *The Australian*. February 10, 2009.

"The Cities: The Price of Optimism." *Time*. August 1, 1969: 39–41.

Cromie, William J. "Cooking Up Quite a Story." *Harvard University Gazette*. June 13, 2002.

Faith, Nicholas. *Blaze*. New York: St. Martin's Press, 1999.

Flint, William. "A History of U.S. Lightships." U.S. Coast Guard website, www.uscg.mil/history/h_lightships.html

Hawley, John Stratton. *Sati: The Blessing and the Curse*. Oxford: Oxford University Press, 1994.

Hibben, Thomas. *The Sons of Vulcan*. Philadelphia: J. B. Lippencott, 1940.

Jones, David E. *An Instinct for Dragons*. New York: Routledge, 2000.

Kelly, J. M. "Fire over Kuwait." *Popular Science*. September 1991: 62–65.

Kelly, Jack. *Gunpowder*. New York: Basic Books, 2004.

Latham, Robert, and William Matthews, eds. *The Diary of Samuel Pepys*. Berkeley: University of California Press, 1972.

Lawson, John A. *A New Voyage to Carolina*. Champaign, IL: Project Gutenberg, 1711.

Levack, Brian P. *The Witch-Hunt in Early Modern Europe*. Harlow, UK: Pearson Education, 1995.

"Lightning: The Shocking Story." National Geographic Kids website, www.nationalgeographic.com/lightning

Lucas, A., and J. R. Harris. *Ancient Egyptian Materials and Industries.* New York: Dover Publications, 1999.

Marley, Karin. "We Can't Stop Playing with our Food." *Maclean's.* August 18, 2005: 36–37.

McBride, Michele. *The Fire That Will Not Die.* Palm Springs, CA: ETC Publications, 1979.

Miller, Ross. *The Great Chicago Fire.* Chicago: University of Illinois Press, 1990.

Newton, David E. *Encyclopedia of Fire.* Westport, CT: Oryx Press, 2002.

Partington, J. R. *A History of Greek Fire and Gunpowder.* Baltimore: The Johns Hopkins University Press, 1999.

Porter, Stephen. *The Great Fire of London.* Phoenix Mill, UK: Sutton Publishing, 1996.

Pyne, Stephen J. *Vestal Fire.* Seattle: University of Washington Press, 1997.
———. *World Fire.* New York: Henry Holt, 1995.

Rehder, J. E. *The Mastery and Uses of Fire in Antiquity.* Montreal: McGill-Queen's University Press, 2000.

Rosi, Mauro, Paulo Papale, Luca Lupi, and Marco Stoppato. *Volcanoes.* Toronto: Firefly Books, 2003.

Rossoti, Hazel. *Fire.* Oxford: Oxford University Press, 1993.

Salisbury, Harrison E. *The Great Black Dragon Fire.* Boston: Little, Brown & Co., 1989.

"Solar Physics." Marshall Space Flight Center website, www.solarscience.msfc.nasa.gov/SunspotCycle.shtml

White, Ellen Emerson. "Profiling Arsonists and Their Motives." *Fire Engineering.* March 1996: 80.

Williams, Peter. *Beacon on the Rock.* Edinburgh: Birlinn, 2001.

Index

About the Author

TANYA LLOYD KYI has been interested in fire ever since she and her friend Michelle worked together on a grade 8 science fair project about lightning. They used a static generator, cotton balls, and a small figurine of a golfer to show how lightning worked. Unfortunately, the cotton-ball clouds turned out to be flammable. The innocent golfer was not only struck by lightning but also somewhat melted by the flames.

Tanya has managed to survive most of her life without setting any more fires, except for one small incident with the Christmas turkey in 2001. She is the author of *Fires!*; *Rescues!*; *Jared Lester: Fifth Grade Jester*; and *The Blue Jean Book*, which won the Christie Harris Illustrated Children's Literature Prize. She lives in Vancouver, BC.

About the Illustrator

ROSS KINNAIRD has illustrated about a dozen books for children. When asked how he comes up with his ideas, he replies that he sits in a bath of warm lemonade with a frozen chicken on his head!

The thing he enjoys most about being an illustrator is visiting schools to talk about books and drawing funny pictures of teachers. He has been to about 150 schools and spoken to thousands of kids.

He loves to travel and has been all over the world, including China, Australia, India, Britain, France, Spain, and Morocco. He lives in New Zealand.